Kip Can Spin

by Clint Campo
illustrated by Hector Borlasca

Practice Decodable 19

McGraw Hill Education

Bothell, WA • Chicago, IL • Columbus, OH • New York, NY

MHEonline.com

Send all inquiries to:
McGraw-Hill Education
8787 Orion Place
Columbus, OH 43240

ISBN: 978-0-02-145018-3
MHID: 0-02-145018-8

Printed in China.

8 9 10 11 12 DSS 27 26 25 24 23

Scott still sits and talks.

Kip sat in the back.

"I spot a clock," said Kip.

"I can spin," said Kip.

Kip did spin—blocks and blocks!

Sad Scott kicks back and sits.